BASKETBALL

AND ITS GREATEST PLAYERS

inside sports

BASKETBALL
AND ITS GREATEST PLAYERS

EDITED BY SHERMAN HOLLAR

Britannica
Educational Publishing

IN ASSOCIATION WITH

ROSEN
EDUCATIONAL SERVICES

Published in 2012 by Britannica Educational Publishing
(a trademark of Encyclopædia Britannica, Inc.)
in association with Rosen Educational Services, LLC
29 East 21st Street, New York, NY 10010.

Distributed exclusively by Rosen Educational Services.
For a listing of additional Britannica Educational Publishing titles, call toll free (800) 237-9932.

First Edition

Britannica Educational Publishing
Michael I. Levy: Executive Editor, Encyclopædia Britannica
J.E. Luebering: Director, Core Reference Group, Encyclopædia Britannica
Adam Augustyn: Assistant Manager, Encyclopædia Britannica

Anthony L. Green: Editor, Compton's by Britannica
Michael Anderson: Senior Editor, Compton's by Britannica
Sherman Hollar: Associate Editor, Compton's by Britannica

Marilyn L. Barton: Senior Coordinator, Production Control
Steven Bosco: Director, Editorial Technologies
Lisa S. Braucher: Senior Producer and Data Editor
Yvette Charboneau: Senior Copy Editor
Kathy Nakamura: Manager, Media Acquisition

Rosen Educational Services
Shalini Saxena: Editor
Nelson Sá: Art Director
Cindy Reiman: Photography Manager
Matthew Cauli: Designer, Cover Design
Introduction by Shalini Saxena

Library of Congress Cataloging-in-Publication Data

Basketball and its greatest players / edited by Sherman Hollar.
    p. cm. — (Inside sports)
"In association with Britannica Educational Publishing, Rosen Educational Services."
Includes bibliographical references and index.
ISBN 978-1-61530-509-4 (library binding)
1. Basketball players—Juvenile literature. I. Hollar, Sherman.
GV885.1.B36 2011
796.323—dc22

                                                                              2010052666

Manufactured in the United States of America

CONTENTS

INTRODUCTION		6
CHAPTER 1	THE GAME OF BASKETBALL	10
CHAPTER 2	HISTORY OF THE GAME	27
CHAPTER 3	WOMEN'S BASKETBALL AND INTERNATIONAL COMPETITION	38
CHAPTER 4	NOTABLE PLAYERS	48

CONCLUSION	84
GLOSSARY	85
FOR MORE INFORMATION	88
BIBLIOGRAPHY	91
INDEX	92

INTRODUCTION

While baseball has long been considered the American national pastime and football the most watched televised sport in the country, basketball—conceived entirely by Massachusetts physical education instructor James Naismith—is also a truly American institution. From casual one-on-one games in a gym to international Olympic-level competitions, "shooting hoops" has come to occupy a unique place on the both the American and international cultural landscapes. This volume examines the history of this much-loved form of recreation and introduces some of the game-changing professional players whose abilities have elevated the artistry of the game.

At first glance, basketball does not seem to be a complicated sport. As its name suggests, the key components of a basketball game are a ball and a basket into which the ball must be thrown in order to score points (the actual peach baskets used in early games were later replaced with the open hoops in use today). However, a number of elements add a certain amount of drama to each game. Within a short amount of time after gaining possession of the ball, each team must attempt to sink a shot into the basket that the opposing team is defending. Various offensive and defensive strategies may be employed throughout the course of a game. The press, for example, is a defensive strategy often used to force the opposition to hurry its movements and to commit errors that result in turnovers.

Originally designed as an indoor game for Naismith's students to play in the winter, basketball has since evolved in many respects. Although it is still enjoyed by students and casual athletes both indoors and out, its national and international appeal has escalated dramatically. The National Basketball Association (NBA) can be credited with much of this change. While it competed with other professional leagues in its early years, it eventually emerged as the primary professional league for male players in the United States and

transformed the game. With increased visibility and popularity both at home and abroad, the NBA's teams and players have sold out arenas and attracted new generations of fans.

With basketball quickly gaining traction around the country after its introduction, it was only a matter of time before women and international players took to the court. Women's teams emerged soon after men's teams, and basketball has thus retained popularity among women nearly as long as it has men. Like the men's game, women's basketball has undergone a number of modifications over the years. The establishment of the Women's

The first basketball court was set up in this Springfield, Mass., gymnasium in 1891 by James Naismith. **Hulton Archive/Getty Images**

National Basketball Association (WNBA) in 1997 as the primary professional league for female players in the United States cemented the presence of women's games on national television and made the game accessible to wider audiences. International teams and players have similarly adopted the game and helped make basketball a global phenomenon.

Although basketball is a team sport that in many ways demands that the whole be greater than the sum of its parts, individual players have been critical to advancing the sport and introducing new moves and dynamics to the game. After all, one can hardly mention basketball without recalling the acrobatics of Michael Jordan, or Air Jordan, as he aptly came to be known. The icons of today—Shaquille O'Neal, Kobe Bryant, LeBron James, to name a few—owe much to the generations of athletes who preceded them and have continued their legacy of innovation in exciting fashion.

From its humble beginnings in a school gym to selling out Madison Square Garden, basketball has endured and evolved immensely in the years since its invention. Still, it retains much of its original character and stands as a testament to the imagination of one teacher as much as it does to the dedication of the remarkable players that have reinvented the idea of skill.

CHAPTER 1

THE GAME OF BASKETBALL

I t could have been called boxball. In the winter of 1891, James Naismith, an instructor at a YMCA training school in Springfield, Mass., asked the janitor to hang a couple of boxes from the gymnasium balcony for an experimental indoor ball game. The game became known as basketball because the janitor, unable to find boxes to make the elevated goals, nailed up two half-bushel peach baskets. Naismith came up with the game in hopes of curing the winter doldrums of his students who had grown bored with the routine of gymnastics and calisthenics. Naismith first experimented with indoor versions of rugby, lacrosse, and other sports, but they proved too violent. The former divinity student eventually struck upon the idea of upright goals that would minimize the force on the ball and

James Naismith, the creator of basketball. **Hulton Archive/ Getty Images**

keep some distance between the players and the actual scoring. Thus the internationally popular game of basketball was born.

HOW THE GAME IS PLAYED

The first basketball games played by James Naismith's students had two nine-man teams and were played with a soccer ball. In the first years of basketball competition, the game was played under a wide range of rules. The number of players varied from 10 to 18, the courts were often irregularly shaped, and baskets were attached to balconies that allowed fans to swat shots from the basket. Within the next decade the familiar rules and equipment of the modern game were established and continued to be modified to enhance the excitement of the competition.

RULES AND EQUIPMENT

The dimensions of the indoor playing floor are 50 feet (15.2 meters) by 94 feet (28.7 meters) for professional and college play. High school courts may be smaller. The international court is 49.2 feet (15 meters) by 92 feet (28 meters). Every court includes a line that divides the court in half, and at

the midpoint of that line is the center circle. Other court markings include the free throw line and lane markings, and a three-point line that is 19 feet 9 inches (6 meters) from the basket in college and high school play and 23 feet 9 inches (7.2 meters) in the National Basketball Association (NBA). At each end of the court is a goal, or basket,

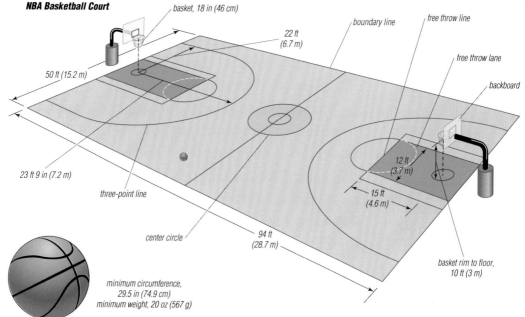

NBA Basketball Court

basket, 18 in (46 cm)

boundary line

free throw line

22 ft (6.7 m)

free throw lane

backboard

50 ft (15.2 m)

23 ft 9 in (7.2 m)

three-point line

12 ft (3.7 m)

15 ft (4.6 m)

center circle

94 ft (28.7 m)

basket rim to floor, 10 ft (3 m)

minimum circumference, 29.5 in (74.9 cm)
minimum weight, 20 oz (567 g)

For NBA competition a basketball court is laid out on a hardwood floor in a gymnasium or other indoor arena. The area at each end of the court marked by the free throw lane and its restraining circle, popularly called the key, is named for its resemblance to a keyhole. The standard dimensions of 94 feet (28.7 meters) in length and 50 feet (15.2 meters) in width may vary in high school and international play. © Merriam-Webster Inc.

10 feet (3 meters) above the floor. The first goals were literally baskets, and a ladder was kept nearby to clear out the basket after each successful goal. When metal baskets were substituted, a pole was needed to poke the ball out of a hole in the bottom. The metal rim of the hoop was not invented until 1906. A bag of braided cord netting was attached to the hoop, and after a score the ball was released by pulling a cord. The current basket is a metal orange ring, 18 inches (46 centimeters) in diameter, with an open net suspended from the rim.

The backboard was introduced in 1895 in order to prevent fans sitting in balconies from interfering with the baskets. The backboard is now an important factor in the game and is used by skilled players to make shooting easier. Backboards are either rectangular or fan-shaped and may be made of any rigid material—usually glass. The soccer balls used in early basketball games were replaced by laced leather balls, then laceless ones, and finally the molded leather- or composition-covered balls in use today. The inflated ball has a grippable, pebbled surface. It measures 29.5 to 30 inches (74.9 to 76 centimeters) in circumference and weighs 20 to 22 ounces (567 to 624 grams).

A modern basketball. © www.istockphoto.com/Jason Lugo

In 1897 the number of players per side for a basketball game was set at five. Typically the five players are a center, two forwards (one power forward and one small forward), and two guards (one point guard and one shooting guard). While there are five players per team on the court at any given time, the total number of players on a team may be higher (no more than 15 in the NBA), and substitutions may occur during the game.

For collegiate, professional, and international games there are three referees, who are assisted by two timekeepers and two scorers. (A single timekeeper and a single scorer may be used if acceptable to the referee.)

The length of the game is regulated according to the age and physical strength of the players. College basketball teams play two 20-minute halves, with a 15-minute rest between halves. If the score is tied at the end of the two halves, play continues for as many five-minute overtime periods as it takes for one team to break the tie. High school teams play four eight-minute periods, with a ten-minute intermission at halftime, plus three-minute overtime periods if needed. NBA games consist of four 12-minute periods with a 20-minute rest between halves. The tie-breaking overtime periods are five minutes long.

The visiting team has the choice of baskets at the start of the game, and the teams change baskets for the second half. Play begins when the referee tosses up the ball between two opposing players, who stand

A player dribbles a ball down a court. **Darryl Bautista © The Rosen Publishing Group and Darryl Bautista**

inside the center circle and jump to tap the ball to a teammate. Other players must stay outside the circle until the ball is tapped.

Each team strives to outscore the other by making as many baskets as possible. Any player may shoot at the basket. A successful shot is a field goal, which counts for two points. If the shot is attempted beyond the three-point line, then the successful shot counts for three points. Successful free throws (unhindered shots at the basket from the free throw line) count for one point each.

A player with possession of the ball must pass or shoot before taking two steps or must start dribbling (bouncing the ball) before taking a second step. The dribble continues until the player touches the ball with both hands at once, permits it to come to rest, or loses control of it. The ball may be batted with the hands, passed, bounced, or rolled in any direction.

When a field goal or free throw attempt fails, play continues. After each successful

The shot clock is displayed above the backboard in a game of college basketball. College teams are required to sink or attempt a shot that makes contact with the rim within 35 seconds of taking control of the ball. Jonathan Daniel/ Getty Images

basket, the team that did not score puts the ball in play from behind the end line at the basket it is defending.

In 1954 the shot clock was introduced in the NBA in order to increase scoring and the pace of the game. The shot clock begins when a team takes possession of the ball. Teams are required to take a shot that is either successful or makes contact with the rim within a set amount of time. The NBA and international leagues have a 24-second clock; college has a 35-second clock. There is no shot clock in high school basketball.

VIOLATIONS AND FOULS

Penalties are given for two general types of offenses—violations and fouls. The most common violations include: running or walking with the ball without dribbling; double dribbling (using both hands at the same time to dribble or stopping and restarting the dribble); and goaltending (interfering with a shot on the ball's downward path into the basket). Other violations include kicking the ball intentionally and, in the case of most American competition, touching the ball while it is on the rim of the basket.

SHOTS FROM THE FIELD

One of the main field shots in the game of basketball is the layup, in which the shooter, while close to the basket, jumps and lays the ball against the backboard so it will rebound into the basket or just lays it over the rim. Away

A player slam-dunks a ball through the hoop.
Shutterstock.com

from the basket, players use a one-hand push shot from a stride, jump, or standing position and a hook shot, which is overhead. The jump shot is a particularly effective offensive weapon, since it is released at the top of the jump, making it difficult to defend. Some players can dunk or slam-dunk the ball, jamming the ball down into the basket.

Most violations are punished by awarding the ball out-of-bounds to the other team.

Fouls may be either personal or technical. Since basketball is theoretically not a body contact sport, a personal foul can result from any physical involvement with an opposing player. Pushing, pulling, bumping, holding, tripping, and charging are all infractions of the rules. A personal foul may be a common foul (neither obvious nor intentional), double foul (in which two opponents commit personal fouls against each other at about the same time), or multiple foul (in which two players on one team commit personal fouls against an opponent at about the same time). A player control foul is a common foul committed by a player while controlling the ball.

The officials call the fouls, penalizing the offending team either by awarding the ball out-of-bounds to its opponents or by

A defending player (right) fouls an offensive player handling the ball.
Darryl Bautista © The Rosen Publishing Group and Darryl Bautista

awarding free throws. If a player is fouled in the act of shooting and misses the basket, he receives two free throws (three, if fouled attempting a three-point shot). If he is fouled in the act of shooting and makes the basket, the score counts and he receives an additional free throw. A high school or college player who commits five personal fouls must leave the game. NBA players are allowed six fouls. When a player is called for a personal foul, the foul is also registered against the team. When a team exceeds its limit—four team fouls per quarter in professional play and six per half in college and high school play—the opposing team receives extra free throws.

A technical foul may be committed by either a player or a nonplayer, such as coaches or spectators. Technical fouls are called against a team for delaying the game, unsportsman-like tactics, illegal substitutions, or illegal time-outs. The penalty throw for a technical foul may be made by any member of the opposing team, which then is usually given possession of the ball out-of-bounds at midcourt.

STYLES OF PLAY

Teams employ different styles of play on both the offensive and defensive ends of

Ryan Kelly (#34) and Kyle Singler (#12) of the Duke Blue Jay-R Strowbridge (#55) of the Oregon Ducks. Jona Getty Images

the court. One of the best-known styles of offensive play is the motion offense. In the motion offense, all the players weave in and out of the area in front of the basket, trying to block defenders and free their teammates for open shots. A common play within the motion offense is the pick-and-roll, in which a player sets a "pick" for a teammate with the

ball by getting in the way of the defender guarding him. If the defender continues to follow the ball handler, the player setting the pick moves, or "rolls," toward the basket and is often able to get open for a pass and shot. Some teams prefer the fast-break style of play that emphasizes pushing the ball quickly toward the offensive end and taking shots before the defense is set.

The two primary styles of defense are zone and man-to-man. In a zone defense, each defensive player guards a certain area on the court. In man-to-man defense, each player guards a specific player on the opposing team. In a combination defense, two or three players guard certain zones while the others play man-to-man defense. The press, which forces the offensive team to move the ball quickly, is used often by a team that is losing toward the end of the game. In employing a press, a team goes all out to try to block and steal the ball from the other team. Most teams use a man-to-man press, a full-court zone press, or a half-court zone press.

CHAPTER 2

HISTORY OF THE GAME

Basketball is the only major sport that is completely American in origin. Following its invention by Naismith in 1891, the game quickly spread through the United States, and the first professional teams emerged in the Northeast at the turn of the 20th century. These teams were instrumental in developing the game, introducing key elements such as the bounce pass and the free throw following a foul. The first professional league was the National Basketball League, which formed in 1898. The early professional games were very physical and often stirred the emotion of fans to such a point that the atmosphere at games was frequently hostile. Chicken wire cages (and later rope netting) was placed around the court to separate players and fans. Even decades after this practice disappeared, basketball players were referred to as "cagers."

THE BARNSTORMING ERA

Three barnstorming professional teams had a major impact on the sport—the Original Celtics, the New York Renaissance (often called the Rens), and the Harlem Globetrotters. Led by 6-foot, 5-inch (1.96-meter) Joe Lapchick, the Original Celtics were formed in New York City and dominated professional play in the 1920s with their switching man-to-man defense and superior passing game. The Celtics, an all-white team, had a memorable clash with the all-black New York Rens in 1925–26 when the two teams split 6 games. Formed by Robert Douglas in

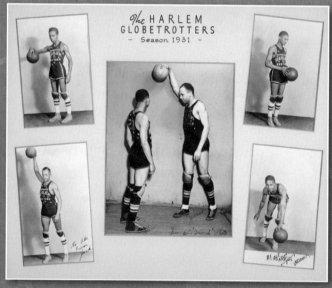

A five-photograph composite shows members of the Harlem Globetrotters team in 1931. Chicago History Museum/Archive Photos/Getty Images

1922, the New York Rens were one of the finest teams of the barnstorming era. In the 1932–33 season, the Rens won 88 consecutive games, and in 1939 they won the World Professional Tournament. The Harlem Globetrotters, an all-black squad founded in 1927 by promoter and coach Abe Saperstein, originally played exhibitions in a Chicago ballroom. By the 1930s the Globetrotters had attracted top black players and were dominating other teams with their superior ball-handling ability. As the games became increasingly lopsided, the team developed its trademark comic style—players spinning the ball on their fingers, head-bouncing it into the basket, dribbling behind the back, and making blind passes—in order to make the games entertaining.

THE EARLY YEARS OF THE NBA

Basketball's premiere league, the NBA, was formed in 1949 when the National Basketball League merged with the Basketball Association of America. The NBA flourished in its early years due in large part to the brilliant play of Minneapolis Lakers center George Mikan. Standing 6 feet 10 inches (2.08 meters), Mikan was the game's first dominant center, and his playing style had an influence on many subsequent big men. In 1950 the NBA

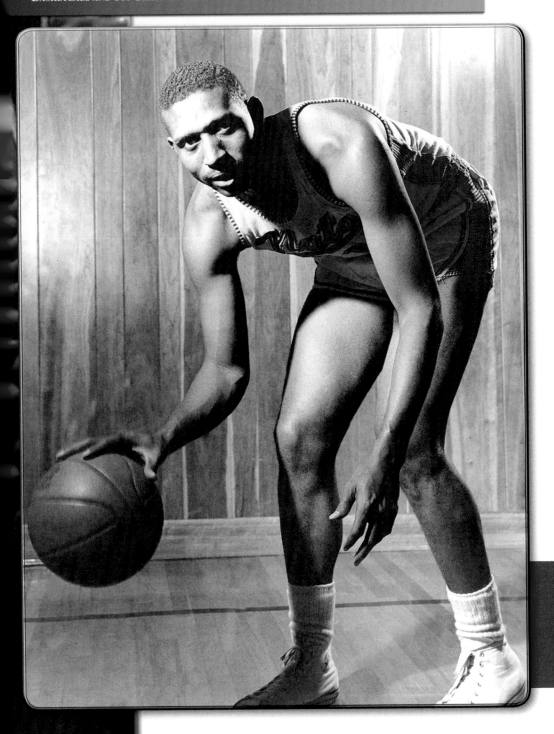

was integrated by African American players Earl Lloyd, Chuck Cooper, and Nathaniel "Sweetwater" Clifton. The NBA was unchallenged as the top basketball league until the American Basketball Association (ABA) emerged in 1967. The ABA introduced the three-point basket and played a more open style of basketball that soon attracted large crowds. The ABA competed with the NBA for top players but eventually collapsed under financial burdens, though four ABA teams were absorbed into the NBA.

A New Era of Superstars

By the early 1980s the NBA was plagued by money-losing franchises, low attendance, and declining television ratings. The league soon rebounded under the leadership of David Stern, NBA commissioner from 1984, who helped transform it into an international entertainment company. Aggressive marketing highlighted star players such as Magic

When Earl Lloyd was selected to play with the Washington Capitols in 1950, he became one of the first black players in the NBA. Here he poses for a photograph after joining the Syracuse Nationals. **NBA Photos/National Basketball Association/Getty Images**

NBA commissioner David Stern (right) gives a ring to Larry Bird of the Boston Celtics during the 1984 Championship ring ceremony. **Dick Raphael/NBAE via Getty Images**

Johnson, Larry Bird, and, especially, Michael Jordan. Other innovations included league limits on player salaries, lucrative broadcast rights for network and cable television, and expanded All-Star Game festivities.

THE NBA TODAY

As of 2011, the NBA had a total of 30 teams organized into Eastern and Western

The Boston Celtics in 2009. The Celtics are one of 15 teams in the NBA's Eastern Conference. **Brian Babineau/NBAE via Getty Images**

conferences and further divided into six divisions. In the Eastern Conference the Atlantic Division comprises the Boston Celtics, the New Jersey Nets (in Newark), the New York Knicks, the Philadelphia 76ers, and the Toronto Raptors; the Central Division is made up of the Chicago Bulls, the Cleveland Cavaliers, the Detroit Pistons, the Indiana Pacers (in Indianapolis), and the Milwaukee (Wisconsin) Bucks; the

The Los Angeles Lakers in 2010. The Lakers are one of 15 teams in the NBA's Western Conference. Andrew D. Bernstein/NBAE via Getty Images

Southeast Division comprises the Atlanta Hawks, the Charlotte (North Carolina) Bobcats, the Miami Heat, the Orlando (Florida) Magic, and the Washington (D.C.) Wizards. In the Western Conference the Southwest Division comprises the Texas-based Dallas Mavericks, Houston Rockets, and San Antonio Spurs, the Memphis

New York City's Madison Square Garden, home of the New York Knicks, is often packed with fans during games, such as this one between the Knicks and the Miami Heat in 2005. Jim McIsaac/Getty Images

(Tennessee) Grizzlies, and the New Orleans Hornets; the Northwest Division is made up of the Denver Nuggets, the Minnesota Timberwolves (in Minneapolis), the Oklahoma City Thunder, the Portland (Oregon) Trail Blazers, and the Utah Jazz (in Salt Lake City); the Pacific Division comprises the Phoenix Suns and the

THE NBDL

In 2001 the NBA launched the National Basketball Development League (NBDL). The NBDL served as a kind of "farm system" for the NBA. Through its first 50 years the NBA did not have an official system of player development or a true minor league system for bringing up young and inexperienced players such as the one that exists in major league baseball. College basketball has been the area from which the NBA did the vast majority of its recruiting. By 2000 this had begun to change somewhat, as players began to be drafted straight out of high school with increasing frequency. In 2005 the NBA instituted a rule stipulating that domestic players must be at least age 19 and have been out of high school for one year to be eligible for the draft, which in effect required players to spend at least one year in college or on an international professional team before coming to the NBA.

California-based Golden State Warriors (in Oakland), Los Angeles Clippers, Los Angeles Lakers, and Sacramento Kings.

The play-offs follow the traditional 82-game schedule, involving 16 teams and beginning in late April. Played as a best-of-seven series, the final pairings stretch into late June. Although basketball is traditionally a winter game, the NBA still fills its arenas and attracts a national television audience in late spring and early summer.

As the popularity of the league grew, player salaries rose to an annual average of more than $5 million by mid-2000s, and some superstars earned more than $20 million yearly. The NBA has a salary cap that limits (at least theoretically, as loopholes allow many teams to exceed the cap) the total amount a team can spend on salaries in any given season.

CHAPTER 3

WOMEN'S BASKETBALL AND INTERNATIONAL COMPETITION

Basketball has always enjoyed great popularity. Within a decade of its invention there were women's teams, professional circuits, and an intercollegiate conference. The game quickly spread to Canada, Europe, and Australia. Today, young people play basketball in grade school, high school, college, and at athletic clubs. In addition to amateur teams, there are professional leagues and independent professional clubs throughout the world.

DEVELOPMENT OF THE WOMEN'S GAME

Women have been playing basketball for almost as long as men. Senda Berenson, a physical education teacher at all-female

Smith College in Northampton, Mass., observed men playing the game at a nearby institution in the early 1890s and decided to try it with her students. Other colleges followed suit, and teams from Stanford University and the University of California at Berkeley met in 1896 for the first women's intercollegiate basketball game.

Although the women's rules at the high school, collegiate, and professional levels today are similar to those for the men's game, this was not the case when the sport

The U.S. women's national team won the gold medal in the 2000 Olympic Games held in Sydney, Australia. M team are pictured during the playing of the national ant D. Bernstein/NBAE via Getty Images

began. Clara Baer, who introduced basketball at the H. Sophie Newcombe College for women in New Orleans, misread a diagram of the court sent to her by James Naismith and restricted the movement of offensive and defensive players to one end of the court. The mistake, however, was quickly embraced as many people considered it unladylike for women to play competitive sports and preferred the limitations placed on movement. Others worried about the health of female athletes and tried to compensate by shortening the time in each play period. Modifications occurred through the years, but the full-court, five-player team did not become standard until the early 1970s.

The International Women's Sports Federation included basketball in its version of the Olympics in 1924. In 1926 the Amateur Athletic Union started sponsoring an annual basketball tournament for women. The World Amateur Basketball Championship for women began in 1953, with the United States team taking the gold medal. A squad from the Soviet Union won the first Olympic gold medal for women's basketball at the 1976 Summer Games in Montreal. U.S. women's teams were crowned Olympic champions in 1984, 1988, 1996, 2000, and 2004.

Women's basketball, and women's sports in general, received a major boost in 1972 with the introduction in the United States of Title IX, a law banning sexual discrimination at educational institutions receiving federal funds. As a result, more high schools fielded women's teams, and opportunities increased for female athletes to receive college scholarships.

Collegiate women's basketball continued to change when control switched from the Association for Intercollegiate Athletics for Women to the National Collegiate Athletic Association (NCAA) in the early 1980s. The NCAA ran the sport more efficiently and increased its visibility, resulting in the attendance figures for women's collegiate basketball games skyrocketing to more than five times their 1982 levels by 2005.

THE RISE OF THE WNBA

Unlike their male counterparts, female hoopsters had little opportunity to play professionally in the United States for some time. An attempt to change this situation came in 1978 with the formation of the Women's Professional Basketball League, but financial losses caused the eight-team league to

Lynette Woodard, the first female member of the Harlem Globetrotters, joins her teammates on the court. **Focus On Sport/Getty Images**

disband after three seasons. Ann Meyers, a former star at the University of California at Los Angeles, signed a one-year contract with the Indiana Pacers of the NBA in 1979, but she did not make the team. In 1985 Lynette Woodard became the first female member of the Harlem Globetrotters, and Olympian Nancy Lieberman became the first woman to play in a men's professional basketball league when she joined the now-defunct

The Los Angeles Sparks, one of 14 teams in the WNBA, in
Vy/NBAE via Getty Images

United States Basketball League in 1986.
Most American women who wanted to play
professionally, however, resorted to travel-
ing overseas to join flourishing leagues in
Europe, South America, Asia, and Australia.
Some chose to stay in the United States to
work in such sports-related fields as coaching and broadcasting.

With the popularity of women's basketball at an all-time high in the United
States following the 1996 Atlanta Olympics,

new efforts were made to establish professional leagues for women. The American Basketball League (ABL), organized with start-up money from private businesspeople, debuted in October 1996 with eight teams. Backed by the powerful NBA, the Women's National Basketball Association (WNBA) tipped off in June 1997. Eight NBA cities were chosen to host WNBA franchises. Unlike the ABL, whose teams played during the traditional basketball season, WNBA teams played during the summer, with post-season semifinal and championship games held at the end of August. This enabled the women to use the same arenas as the men and helped the teams receive television exposure by not having to compete against collegiate and professional men's basketball. Cable stations chose to show many weekday games, and the league received network coverage on the weekends. The success of the WNBA allowed it to draw better talent and it forced the ABL to fold in 1998. By 2006 the WNBA had grown to 14 teams.

INTERNATIONAL COMPETITION

Despite its American origins, basketball has become a sport without boundaries. The

Fédération Internationale de Basketball, the world governing body of basketball, was established in 1932, and the sport made its official Olympic debut in 1936. World

D'or Fischer (left), an American playing for Spain's Real Madrid, attempts to defend against Theodoros Papaloukas of Greece's Olympiakos. **Pierre-Philippe Marcou/AFP/Getty Images**

championships were established in 1950 for men and in 1953 for women. Professional leagues developed in Europe, Asia, and Australia, and in the second half of the 20th century, many American players, unable to land a spot on an NBA team, traveled overseas to play professionally. The United States dominated international play for decades, but the quality of play outside the United States improved dramatically in the 1970s, and international competition was no longer one-sided. In the 1980s U.S. colleges began to actively recruit players from overseas, and during that

Yao Ming of the Houston Rockets slam-dunks in a 2003 game against the Los Angeles Lakers. **Brian Bahr/Getty Images**

time players from Europe—such as Detlef Schrempf of Germany and Drazen Petrovic of Yugoslavia—became key contributors on NBA teams. Today, players from Africa, Asia, Europe, and Australia are on NBA rosters. In 2002 Yao Ming of China became the first non-American player to be selected as the top pick in the NBA draft.

CHAPTER 4

NOTABLE PLAYERS

While most of the original rules of basketball posted by James Naismith a century ago have endured, style and performance give the modern game a wholly different look. Over the course of the game's development, superstars of each generation perfected moves that earlier players could never have imagined—Wilt Chamberlain's finger roll, Kareem Abdul-Jabbar's sky hook, Julius Erving's slam dunk, Magic Johnson's no-look pass, Michael Jordan's incredible hang time. The careers of these and other influential players are discussed on the following pages.

EARLY NBA PLAYERS

George Mikan

In a 1950 Associated Press poll, George Mikan was selected as the greatest basketball

George Mikan of the Minneapolis Lakers, wearing his signature goggles, shows off his hook shot. **NBA Photos/NBAE via Getty Images**

player of the first half of the 20th century. He was the first of the outstanding big men in the post-World War II professional game. Born in Joliet, Ill., on June 18, 1924, he played center for the Minneapolis Lakers from 1947 through 1954 and for a brief stint in the 1955–56 season, scoring 11,764 points in 520 regular-season games for an average of 22.6 points a game. In 91 playoff games, he scored 2,141 points for a 23.5 average. In an era when the professional game was known for its rough play, the lanky and nearsighted Mikan, wearing thick protective goggles, hardly looked the part of a basketball star. However, despite numerous broken bones and countless cuts and bruises, Mikan thrived in the sport. With Mikan at center, the Lakers won six championships from 1947–48 through 1953–54 (1950–51 season excepted). After retiring as a player, he coached the Lakers for part of the 1957–58 season and later served as commissioner of the ABA. Mikan was inducted into the Basketball Hall of Fame in 1959. He died on June 1, 2005, in Scottsdale, Ariz.

Bob Cousy

Known as "Houdini of the Hardwood," Bob Cousy dazzled fans with his dribbling skill and behind-the-back passes. One of the game's great ball-handling guards, he was adept both at scoring and at playmaking. Born in New York, N.Y., on Aug. 9, 1928, he starred at the College of the Holy Cross before breaking into the NBA. During his career with the Boston Celtics from 1950 to 1963, he led the NBA in assists for eight consecutive years, his one-game record of 28 assists (1959) standing until 1978. Teamed with talented players such as Bill Russell, Bill Sharman, and K.C. Jones, Cousy adopted the competitive spirit of his coach Red Auerbach and directed the Celtics' play in six championship seasons (1957, 1959–63). After he left the Celtics, Cousy coached the Boston College Eagles from 1963 to 1969 and the NBA's Cincinnati/Kansas City Royals from 1969 to 1974. From 1975 to 1979 he served as commissioner of the American Soccer League and later became a marketing consultant and part-time television commentator for the Celtics. He was elected to the Basketball Hall of Fame in 1970.

Bill Russell

Standing 6 feet 10 inches (2.08 meters) tall, Bill Russell set standards by which other exceptionally tall players were judged. On

five occasions he was voted the Most Valuable Player in the NBA, and he was selected by the Associated Press as the outstanding professional basketball player of the 1960s. Today many regard him as the best defensive center ever to play the game. Born in Monroe, La., on Feb. 12, 1934, Russell played on the gold medal-winning U.S. Olympic team in 1956 and for the Boston Celtics from 1956 through 1969. With Russell turning shot-blocking into an art form, Boston dominated the NBA for more than a decade. He helped lead the Celtics to 9 championships (1957, 1959–66) in 10 seasons. The team won two more championships (1968–69) with Russell as player and coach. Russell was the first African American to coach a major professional U.S. sports team. He later coached the Seattle SuperSonics from 1973 to 1977 and the Sacramento Kings from 1987 to 1988 and served the Kings briefly as vice-president of operations from 1988 to 1989. Russell was enshrined in the Basketball Hall of Fame in 1975.

WILT CHAMBERLAIN

The press nicknamed him Wilt the Stilt, but he preferred to be called the Big Dipper. Playing center, Wilt Chamberlain was the first outstanding 7-foot (2.13-meter) player in basketball and is still considered by some the greatest offensive player in the history of the game.

Wilton Norman Chamberlain was born in Philadelphia on Aug. 21, 1936. He played two years at the University of Kansas and one season with the Harlem Globetrotters before joining the Philadelphia (later, San Francisco) Warriors of the NBA in 1959. After only one season with the Warriors, he was named the league's Most Valuable Player. During the 1961–62 season he claimed three NBA records when he scored 4,029 points in 80 regular-season games, reached an average of 50.4 points a game, and scored 100 points in a single game. Among Chamberlain's signature moves were the finger roll and fadeaway jump shot.

In the middle of the 1964–65 season Chamberlain was traded to the Philadelphia 76ers. In 1966 he became the second NBA player to attain a career total of 20,000 points, and the next season he led his team to the NBA title and reached a record 68.3 shooting average. Before the 1968–69 season, Chamberlain was traded to the Los Angeles Lakers. In 1968 he reached a record 25,000 career points and became the first center to lead the league in assists. Chamberlain's

powerful presence drove the Lakers to the 1972 NBA title and helped them win a record 33 consecutive victories. When he retired in 1973, he had a record total of 23,924 rebounds and 31,419 points. He was named to the Basketball Hall of Fame in 1978. Chamberlain died on Oct. 12, 1999, in Los Angeles.

OSCAR ROBERTSON

Known as the Big O, Oscar Robertson was long considered the best all-around player in NBA history. Born on Nov. 24, 1938, he grew up in Indianapolis, Ind., where he led Crispus Attucks High School to two state championships. In 1956 he received an athletic scholarship to the University of Cincinnati and became the first African American to play basketball there. In three seasons of collegiate basketball, he averaged 33.8 points per game and helped the Cincinnati Bearcats twice reach the final four of the NCAA tournament. In 1960 he won a gold medal in Rome as a member of the U.S. Olympic team.

Wilt Chamberlain (center) of the Los Angeles Lakers attempts a shot in a game against the Seattle SuperSonics. Wen Roberts/AFP/ Getty Images

That same year he began his professional career as a guard with the Cincinnati Royals. A superior ball handler, he led the league in assists six times. He was named the NBA Most Valuable Player for the 1963–64 season, in which he averaged 31.4 points, 9.9 rebounds, and 11 assists per game. He was traded to the Milwaukee Bucks in 1970 and, with Kareem Abdul-Jabbar, won four Midwest division titles for the Bucks, as well as the NBA championship in 1971. Robertson retired from the NBA in 1974 with 26,710 career points (25.7 per game), 7,804 rebounds (7.5 average), and 9,887 assists (an NBA record at the time). He was elected to the Basketball Hall of Fame in 1979.

RECENT NBA LEGENDS

KAREEM ABDUL-JABBAR

His extraordinary height of 7 feet 2 inches (2.18 meters) combined with extraordinary skills enabled Kareem Abdul-Jabbar to dominate the game of basketball throughout the 1970s and early '80s. He was known for his excellent shooting touch and wide range of graceful post moves, including his sweeping, nearly indefensible sky hook.

Kareem Abdul-Jabbar of the Los Angeles Lakers shoots a graceful sky hook in a game against the Dallas Mavericks. Mike Powell/ Getty Images

Abdul-Jabbar was born Ferdinand Lewis Alcindor, Jr., on April 16, 1947, in New York City. He adopted the better-known Arabic name in 1971, six years after he joined the Black Muslim movement. As a high school basketball player, Lew Alcindor led his team to a 95–6 record and scored 2,067 points, a New York City record for three years. He received more than 100 offers of college scholarships and chose the University of California at Los Angeles (UCLA), which he led to three consecutive NCAA championships.

Upon graduation from UCLA, he was drafted by the Milwaukee Bucks. He continued to play spectacularly at the center position, earning rookie of the year honors in 1970. In 1975 Abdul-Jabbar was traded to the Los Angeles Lakers. He helped the Lakers win the NBA championship in 1980, 1982, 1985, 1987, and 1988. In 1989, the year of his retirement, he became the first player to score more than 38,000 points.

Away from the basketball court, Abdul-Jabbar has earned recognition as a writer. His autobiography, *Giant Steps*, was published in 1983. In addition to his own experiences, he has written on the African American experience, including *Black Profiles in Courage: A Legacy of African American Achievement* (1996; with Alan Steinberg).

JULIUS ERVING

Basketball great Julius Erving, better known as Dr. J., once said of his amazing airborne moves: "It's easy once you learn how to fly." His flights quickly made him one of basketball's all-time top scorers.

Julius Winfield Erving was born in Hempstead, N.Y., on Feb. 22, 1950. In his first year at the University of Massachusetts, he broke records for scoring and rebounding. He left the university in 1971 after his junior year to sign a contract as a forward with the Virginia Squires of the ABA.

In 1973 Erving moved to the New York Nets and, with an average of 27.4 points and 10.7 rebounds per game, led them to the ABA title. Sports enthusiasts believe that when the NBA absorbed the ABA in 1976, it was primarily to get Erving, who joined the Philadelphia 76ers. His first years in Philadelphia were frustrating because the 76er style of play and tendinitis in his knees limited him. But by the 1979–80 season

conditions had changed, and Erving was averaging 26.9 points a game. Erving led the 76ers to the NBA finals four times, including their 1983 championship win.

Erving changed the idea of the way the game of basketball should be played. His airborne feats popularized the slam dunk. His ability to block shots and rebound, as well as pass and handle the ball skillfully, encouraged faster and flashier playing.

Erving's honors included being named ABA Most Valuable Player in 1974, 1975, and 1976, NBA Most Valuable Player in 1981, and numerous elections to ABA and NBA all-star teams. Before his retirement after the 1986–87 season, Erving became only the third player to score 30,000 points in a professional career.

LARRY BIRD

The superstar of the Boston Celtics during the 1980s, Larry Bird had a talent for breathing life into tired basketball organizations. In addition to transforming the Celtics into a championship team, he also helped

Larry Bird of the Boston Celtics attempts a shot during a game. **Getty Images**

rejuvenate the sport's popularity worldwide. Bird is considered one of the greatest pure shooters of all time.

Larry Joe Bird was born on Dec. 7, 1956, in a small rural community near French Lick, Ind. The self-described Hick from French Lick, Bird almost did not play college basketball. Although he was recruited by coach Bobby Knight of Indiana University in 1975, the homesick teenager, overwhelmed by the demands of university life, hitchhiked home after only 3½ weeks at school. A year later, he was recruited to play basketball for Indiana State University in Terre Haute, where he became an immediate phenomenon. In his senior year, Bird led the team into the 1978–79 NCAA championship game with a 33–0 season record. The contest between Bird's Indiana State and Magic Johnson's Michigan State foreshadowed the professional rivalry that would electrify the NBA in the 1980s. Indiana State lost the championship game to Michigan State, but Bird defeated Johnson in the vote for college player of the year.

In 1979 Bird signed a contract with the ailing Boston Celtics, the team that he would stay with for his entire professional career. Leading the team in scoring, rebounding, steals, and minutes played, Bird sparked one of the greatest single-season turnarounds in NBA history. The Celtics improved from a record of 29–53 in 1978–79 to a division-leading record of 61–21 in 1979–80. Although Johnson's Los Angeles Lakers won the 1980 championship, Bird was voted NBA rookie of the year. He went on to lead the Celtics to three NBA championships (1981, 1984, and 1986). Bird also won three consecutive league Most Valuable Player (MVP) awards (1984–86), the first noncenter to do so.

Bird retired in 1993 with career averages of 24.3 points per game and 10 rebounds per game. In 1998 he was elected to the Basketball Hall of Fame. He became the head coach of the Indiana Pacers in 1997 and was named coach of the year after his first season. Bird resigned in 2000 and became the Pacers' president of basketball operations in 2003.

Magic Johnson

Magic Johnson led the Los Angeles Lakers to five NBA championships in the 1980s. Standing 6 feet 9 inches (2.06 meters) tall, he was exceptionally tall for a point guard and was able to use his size to rebound and score inside. However, he was best known for his creative passing and expert floor leadership.

Earvin Johnson, Jr., was born in Lansing, Mich., on Aug. 14, 1959, the sixth of ten children. He got his start playing basketball on the playgrounds of Lansing. As a senior he led the Everett High School team to the Michigan Class A championship. After a particularly amazing display of basketball skill, during which he scored 36 points, grabbed 18 rebounds, and had 16 assists, a Lansing sportswriter christened him Magic. The hometown Michigan State University wooed the All-Stater in 1977. During his sophomore year at Michigan State, he led the Spartans to the NCAA championship—handing Larry Bird and Indiana State its only defeat of that season.

Johnson was drafted by the Los Angeles Lakers in 1979. With Magic leading the team, the Lakers won the NBA championship in 1980, 1982, 1985, 1987, and 1988. He was chosen play-off MVP three times (1980, 1982, and 1987) and was the first rookie to be so named. He was the league's MVP three times (1987, 1989, and 1990), and he helped lead the U.S. team to a basketball gold medal at the

Magic Johnson of the Los Angeles Lakers dribbles a ball down the court during a 1987 game. **Rick Stewart/Getty Images**

1992 Olympics in Barcelona, Spain. His 9,921 career assists set an NBA record (broken by John Stockton in 1995).

With his dazzling smile, style, and blind passes, Johnson was among those credited with professional basketball's surge in popularity in the 1980s. The sports world was stunned on Nov. 7, 1991, when Johnson announced his immediate retirement from professional basketball due to HIV infection. Later he served briefly as head coach of the Lakers (1994), and he returned as a player for a portion of the 1995–96 season. Johnson went on to become a successful entrepreneur and a noted HIV/AIDS activist. He was elected to the Basketball Hall of Fame in 2002.

Michael Jordan

Both literally and figuratively, Michael Jordan soared higher than any NBA guard before him. His extraordinary leaping ability and acrobatic maneuvers inspired his

Michael Jordan of the Chicago Bulls demonstrates one of his storied leaping maneuvers as he seeks to score against the Charlotte Hornets in a 1995 game. Jonathan Daniel/Getty Images

nickname, "Air Jordan." He was the NBA's top scorer for a record-breaking 10 seasons. Also outstanding at defense, Jordan was one of the greatest all-around players in the history of the game.

Michael Jeffrey Jordan was born on Feb. 17, 1963, in Brooklyn, N.Y., but he grew up in Wilmington, N.C. Although he was cut from the varsity basketball team in his sophomore year of high school, he later became one of the team's star players. Jordan earned a scholarship to the University of North Carolina at Chapel Hill, where he helped lead the school's basketball team to the NCAA championship during his freshman year. In both his sophomore and junior years, he was named the NCAA college player of the year. After his junior year he left to join the NBA and was drafted by the Chicago Bulls.

In his first season with the Bulls, the 6-foot-6-inch (1.98-meter) Jordan averaged 28.2 points per game and was named rookie of the year. Jordan won seven consecutive scoring titles from the 1986–87 season through the 1992–93 season. He led the Bulls to three consecutive NBA championships, in 1991, 1992, and 1993. He also led the U.S. basketball team to a gold medal in both the 1984 and 1992 Olympic Games.

Saying that he did not have "anything else to prove," Jordan retired from professional basketball in October 1993. In 1994 he signed to play for a minor league baseball team, but after one season he decided to return to basketball. He rejoined the Bulls late in their 1994–95 season. After leading the team to three more championships in 1996, 1997, and 1998, Jordan retired for the second time in January 1999.

In 2000 Jordan bought a share of the Washington Wizards, but he soon wanted to return to the court. He gave up his ownership position with the Wizards in 2001 in order to play on the team. In the 2002–03 season he became the first player in NBA history age 40 years or older to score more than 40 points in a game. Jordan's final retirement from basketball came in May 2003.

Jordan was named the NBA's Most Valuable Player in 1988, 1991, 1992, 1996, and 1998. At the time of his retirement in 2003, Jordan ranked third in career scoring, with a total of 32,292 points, behind Kareem Abdul-Jabbar and Karl Malone. Jordan's scoring average of 30.12 points per game was the highest in league history. Jordan became part owner of the NBA's Charlotte Bobcats in 2006 and took over control of the team as its majority owner in 2010; he was the first former NBA player to become a majority owner of one of the league's teams. Jordan was inducted into the Basketball Hall of Fame in 2009.

CURRENT NBA PLAYERS

SHAQUILLE O'NEAL

With his intimidating size and outstanding skills, Shaquille O'Neal overwhelmed the competition in the NBA. A 7-foot-1-inch (2.16-meter) center who weighed at least 315 pounds (142.9 kilograms), "Shaq" was nevertheless an agile athlete. Along with teammate Kobe Bryant and coach Phil Jackson, O'Neal led the Los Angeles Lakers to three consecutive NBA championships (2000–02).

Shaquille Rashaun O'Neal was born on March 6, 1972, in Newark, N.J. At age 13 O'Neal, already 6 feet 6 inches (1.98 meters) tall, met Louisiana State University (LSU) head basketball coach Dale Brown, who made an early pitch for O'Neal to join his team. O'Neal ultimately chose LSU, where he became a hot prospect for the pros. As the first pick of the 1992 NBA draft, he was signed by the Orlando Magic to a seven-year,

Shaquille O'Neal of the Cleveland Cavaliers controls the ball while Brad Miller of the Chicago Bulls attempts to defend against him.
Gregory Shamus/Getty Images

40-million-dollar contract, becoming the highest-paid rookie in the NBA. O'Neal went on to be chosen NBA rookie of the year.

After four years with the Magic, O'Neal was lured to join the Lakers in 1996. Under coach Phil Jackson's guidance, O'Neal developed into more of a team player, paying greater attention to his defense and rebounding. In 2000 the Lakers won the NBA championship, and O'Neal was named MVP of the regular season, the All-Star Game, and the NBA finals. The Lakers captured the NBA title again in 2001 and 2002. O'Neal was named the MVP of the finals for both years. The Lakers returned to the NBA finals in 2004 but were defeated. Soon thereafter the team underwent major changes, chief among them a trade that sent O'Neal to the Miami Heat. O'Neal helped lead that team to its first NBA championship, in 2006.

In February 2008 O'Neal was traded to the Phoenix Suns. His playing style did not mix well with the Suns' up-tempo game, however, and—despite having had a very solid 2008–09 season—he was traded to the Cleveland Cavaliers in June 2009. Following the completion of the 2009–10 season, O'Neal signed a two-year contract to play with the Boston Celtics.

One of the most prolific scorers in the history of the NBA, Kobe Bryant helped lead the Los Angeles Lakers to five NBA championships (2000–02, 2009–10).

Kobe Bean Bryant was born on Aug. 23, 1978, in Philadelphia, Pa. Bryant—whose father, Joe Bryant, spent eight seasons in the NBA—played basketball at Lower Merion High School in Ardmore, Pa., where he earned national player of the year honors before opting to forgo college and enter the 1996 NBA draft. Chosen by the Charlotte Hornets with the 13th overall pick in the draft, Bryant was traded to the Lakers and soon proved his merit with the team. In just his second season, he was selected for the NBA All-Star Game, becoming the league's youngest-ever all-star.

Under the leadership of Phil Jackson, who became coach of the Lakers in 1999, Bryant, a shooting guard, and his all-star teammate Shaquille O'Neal, a center, meshed into a remarkably effective combination, and by the time Bryant was 23, the Lakers had won three consecutive NBA championships. The Lakers returned to the NBA finals in 2004 but were upset by the Detroit Pistons. O'Neal

Kobe Bryant of the Los Angeles Lakers celebrates a 2000 Lakers victory against the Seattle SuperSonics. Dan Levine/AFP/Getty Images

subsequently was traded to the Miami Heat, and Bryant emerged as the team's sole leader. He led the league in scoring during the 2005–06 and 2006–07 seasons. In 2008 he was named the league's MVP for the first time in his career; he also starred on the U.S. men's basketball team that captured the gold medal at the Olympic Games in Beijing. In 2009 he won his fourth NBA title as the Lakers decisively defeated the Orlando Magic 4 games to 1 in the finals. Bryant averaged 32.4 points per game in the series and was named the finals MVP. In 2009–10 he was once more named NBA finals MVP after the Lakers defeated the Boston Celtics in a seven-game series.

LeBron James

After entering the NBA directly from high school in 2003, LeBron James quickly established himself as one of the league's superstars. An extraordinarily versatile small forward who was capable of playing multiple positions, James was selected as the NBA's MVP in 2009 and 2010, becoming only the 10th player in NBA history to have earned that honor in consecutive seasons.

LeBron Raymone James was born on Dec. 30, 1984, in Akron, Ohio. In high school, he

LeBron James (right) of the Cleveland Cavaliers and NBA MVP in 2009 receives his trophy from NBA commissioner David Stern. **Gregory Shamus/Getty Images**

was named Ohio's Mr. Basketball three times. In his senior season, he was the consensus national high school player of the year before being chosen by the Cleveland Cavaliers as the first overall pick of the 2003 NBA draft.

James made an immediate impact on the Cavaliers, leading the team in scoring, steals, and minutes played during the 2003–04 season en route to claiming the NBA's rookie of the year award. He was named to the NBA All-Star team for the first time in 2005, and in 2007 he guided Cleveland to the franchise's first berth in the NBA finals. Although James posted a spectacular average of 25 points, 8 rebounds, and 8 assists per game throughout the play-offs that year, the Cavaliers were swept in the finals by the San Antonio Spurs.

During the 2007–08 season, James led the NBA in scoring with an average of 30 points per game and became the youngest player in league history to tally 10,000 career points. The following season he piloted the Cavaliers to a team-record 66 regular-season wins. During both the 2008–09 and 2009–10 seasons, James continued to display his prolific scoring ability, averaging 28.4 and 29.7 points per game, respectively. In addition to his achievements in the NBA, James was a member of the U.S. men's Olympic basketball teams that won the bronze medal at the 2004 Games and the gold medal at the 2008 Games.

At the end of the 2009–10 season James became arguably the most sought-after free agent in NBA history when his contract with the Cavaliers expired. In an unprecedented hour-long television special on the ESPN sports cable network, James announced his decision to sign with the Miami Heat.

Nancy Lieberman of the U.S. women's national team. Tim DeFrisco/
Getty Images

WNBA PLAYERS

Nancy Lieberman

A pioneer in women's basketball, Nancy Lieberman recorded several unprecedented accomplishments in a playing career that spanned three decades.

Born July 1, 1958, in Brooklyn, N.Y., Lieberman garnered attention in the male-dominated New York basketball scene with her natural ability and court savvy. She entered Old Dominion University in Virginia in 1976 and led the school to consecutive Association for Intercollegiate Athletics for Women championships in 1978–79 and 1979–80. An extraordinarily quick point guard, she became known for her precision passing and accurate shooting touch, which enabled her to average 18.1 points per game over her four-year collegiate career. At the international level, she helped lead the United States to a gold medal in the 1975 Pan American Games. She was also a member of the silver-medal-winning 1976 U.S. Olympic team; she made the 1980 team as well, but the squad did not compete because of an American boycott of the Games.

In 1980 Lieberman was the number-one draft pick of the Dallas Diamonds of the Women's Basketball League (WBL), a fledgling women's professional league that folded in 1982. In 1984 Lieberman was again the first draft pick of a newly created professional circuit, the Women's American Basketball Association (WABA). Because fan interest for a women's professional league still was not strong enough to generate financial success, however, the WABA was also short-lived.

Reluctant to leave the United States for Europe, where she had several offers to play professionally, Lieberman continued to look for new opportunities at home. In 1986 she became the first woman to play in a men's professional league, the United States Basketball League, with the Springfield Fame. In 1988 Lieberman was chosen by the Washington Generals to play against the Harlem Globetrotters, making her the first woman to participate in a Harlem Globetrotters world tour. Approaching the age of 40 but still a talented player, she joined the Phoenix Mercury of the newly formed WNBA in 1996.

Outside of her basketball career, Lieberman established her own sports marketing company and became an accomplished broadcaster and a well-known public speaker. She was inducted into the Basketball Hall of Fame in 1996.

CYNTHIA COOPER

The first MVP of the WNBA was Cynthia Cooper of the Houston Comets. In the WNBA's inaugural 1996–97 season, Cooper led the league in scoring while guiding the Comets to the championship. She was named MVP of both the regular season and the playoffs that year.

Born in Chicago, Ill., on April 14, 1963, Cooper was raised in the Watts section of Los Angeles. She began playing organized basketball at age 16 and quickly took to the sport. She earned a scholarship to the University of Southern California, where she played in the shadow of Cheryl Miller while helping the team to national championships in 1983 and 1984. After college Cooper played professionally in Europe, primarily for a team in Parma, Italy, where she blossomed into a potent scorer and a tenacious defender. She was a member of the 1988 U.S. national team that won the gold medal at the Olympic Games in Seoul, South Korea.

By the end of the WNBA's inaugural season, Cooper had established herself as the league's first great player. Along with star teammates Sheryl Swoopes and Tina Thompson, Cooper led the Comets to titles in 1998, 1999, and 2000, each time being recognized as the MVP of the play-offs. She was named the league MVP for the second time in 1998. Cooper retired in 2000 and became the head coach of the WNBA's Phoenix Mercury the following year. She returned to playing basketball in 2003, again with the Comets, and permanently retired from the game in 2004 with WNBA career per-game averages of 21 points, 4.9 assists, 3.3 rebounds, and 1.56 steals. Cooper was named the women's basketball head coach at Prairie View (Texas) A&M University in 2005. She was enshrined in the Basketball Hall of Fame in 2010.

Cynthia Cooper of the Houston Comets shoots a layup in a 2000 game against the New York Liberty. **Ronald Martinez/Getty Images**

CONCLUSION

B y the early 21st century, basketball had developed into a truly global game. In the United States, it was firmly established at the forefront of the sporting scene, alongside such traditional leaders as baseball and football, and in numerous other countries around the world, the game continued to grow steadily both in popularity and importance. Interest in the game has deepened over the years as a result of increased exposure via network and cable television coverage. More importantly, however, it is the nature of the game of itself—its fast and exciting pace, creative and intricate styles of play, frequently dramatic and high-scoring contests, and the skills and athleticism demanded of players at the highest levels— that ensures that the sport of basketball will always have a broad appeal.

assist The action (as a throw or pass) of a player who enables a teammate to make a basket.

barnstorm To travel from place to place staging games.

berth Placement in an athletic tournament or contest.

calisthenics Free body exercises performed with varying degrees of intensity and rhythm that employ such motions as bending, stretching, and jumping, as well as such specialized movements as push-ups, sit-ups, and chin-ups.

championship A contest held to determine the winning team of a season; the final game of the play-offs.

center Player on a basketball team who usually plays near the basket and is typically the tallest person on the team.

draft A system whereby exclusive rights to selected new players are apportioned among professional teams.

dribble To bounce a ball by hand.

forward A player in basketball who plays at the front of his team's formation near the basket at which his team is attempting to score.

free throw An unhindered shot in basketball made from behind a set line and awarded because of a foul by an opponent.

guard A player stationed in the back court in basketball.

hook shot A shot in basketball made usually while standing sideways to the basket by swinging the ball up in an arc with the far hand.

jump shot A shot in basketball made by jumping into the air and releasing the ball with one or both hands at the peak of the jump.

layup A shot in basketball made from near the basket usually by playing the ball off the backboard.

pick-and-roll A basketball play in which a player sets a screen between a ball-handling teammate and a defender from the opposing team and then cuts toward the basket for a pass.

play-off games A series of contests played after the end of the regular season to determine the teams that will compete in the championship game.

point guard A guard in basketball who is chiefly responsible for running the offense.

power forward A basketball forward whose size and strength are used primarily in controlling play near the basket.

press An aggressive pressuring defense in basketball employed against the opposing team often over the entire court area.

prolific Marked by abundant inventiveness or productivity.

shooting guard A guard in basketball whose chief role is as an outside shooter.

slam dunk A shot in basketball made by jumping high into the air and throwing the ball down through the basket.

small forward A basketball forward who is usually smaller than a power forward and whose play is characterized by quickness and scoring ability.

Canada Basketball (CB)
1 Westside Drive, Suite 11
Toronto, ON M9C 1B2
Canada
(416) 614-8037
Web site: http://www.basketball.ca
CB is the national governing body of amateur basketball in Canada. The site
provides information on teams and players throughout the country as well as the
Long-Term Athlete Development Model.

Canadian Colleges Athletic Association
(CCAA)
St. Lawrence College
2 Belmont Street, Windmill Point
Cornwall, ON K6H 4Z1
Canada
(613) 937-1508
Web site: http://www.ccaa.ca
The CCAA provides information on college
athletics throughout Canada as well as
rankings, scores, and regulations.

The National Basketball Association (NBA)
645 Fifth Avenue
New York, NY 10022
(212) 407-8000
Web site: http://www.nba.com

The NBA site provides information on everything from player statistics to game schedules to the history and rules of the NBA. Information on the NBDL and the WNBA is also available.

The National Collegiate Athletic
    Association (NCAA)
700 W. Washington Street
P.O. Box 6222
Indianapolis, IN 46206
(317) 917-6222
Web site: http://www.ncaa.org
The NCAA site provides information on college athletics in the United States and addresses issues facing student athletes. It also offers information on NCAA-sponsored scholarships for students and post-graduates.

USA Basketball
5465 Mark Dabling Boulevard
Colorado Springs, CO 80918
(719) 590-4800
Web site: http://www.usabasketball.com
USA Basketball is the national governing body of basketball in the United States. The site provides information on men's and women's teams throughout

the country as well as the various international competitions in which they compete.

The Women's National Basketball
 Association (WNBA)
645 Fifth Avenue
New York, NY 10022
(212) 407-8000
Web site: http://www.wnba.com
The WNBA site provides information on
 player stats, game schedules, and the
 official history and rules of the WNBA.
 Information on the WNBA's outreach
 program and a glossary of relevant terms
 are also available.

WEB SITES

Due to the changing nature of Internet links, Rosen Educational Services has developed an online list of Web sites related to the subject of this book. This site is updated regularly. Please use this link to access the list:

http://www.rosenlinks.com/spor/bskt

Anderson, Dave. *The Story of Basketball*, rev. ed. (Morrow, 1997).

Bird, Larry, and MacMullan, Jackie. *Bird Watching: On Playing and Coaching the Game I Love* (Warner Books, 2000).

Fleder, Rob. *The Basketball Book* (Time Books, 2007).

Gifford, Clive. *Basketball* (PowerKids Press, 2009).

Lannin, Joanne. *A History of Basketball for Girls and Women* (Lerner Sports, 2000).

Mullin, Chris and Coleman, Brian. *Basketball* (DK, 2000).

Ramen, Fred. *Basketball: Rules, Tips, Strategy, and Safety* (Rosen Central, 2007).

Steen, Sandra, and Steen, Susan. *Take It to the Hoop: 100 Years of Women's Basketball* (Twenty-First Century Books, 2003).

Thomas, Keltie. *How Basketball Works* (Maple Tree Press, 2005).

Thomas, Ron, and Herran, Joe. *Getting Into Basketball* (Chelsea House Publishers, 2006).

A

Abdul-Jabbar, Kareem, 48, 56–59, 69
All-Star Game, 32, 72, 73
American Basketball Association (ABA), 31, 50, 59, 60
American Basketball League (ABL), 44
Atlanta Hawks, 34
Auerbach, Red, 51

B

backboard, about the, 14
Baer, Clara, 40
ball, about the, 14
barnstorming teams, 28–29
basket, about the, 13–14
basketball
  court/equipment for, 12–14
  history of, 10–12, 27–37
  integration of, 29–31
  rules of, 15–20
  styles of play, 24–26
  types of shots, 21–22
  violations and fouls, 20–24
Basketball Association of America, 29

Basketball Hall of Fame, 50, 51, 52, 55, 56, 63, 66, 70, 81, 83
Berenson, Senda, 38–39
Bird, Larry, 32, 60–63, 65
Boston Celtics, 33, 51, 52, 60, 62–63, 72, 75
Brown, Dale, 70
Bryant, Kobe, 70, 73–75

C

Chamberlain, Wilt, 48, 52–55
Charlotte Bobcats, 34, 69–70
Chicago Bulls, 33, 68, 69
Cincinnati Royals, 51, 56
Cleveland Cavaliers, 33, 72, 76–77
Clifton, Nathaniel "Sweetwater," 31
college basketball
  court for, 12, 13
  fouls and, 24
  international players and, 46
  recruiting for NBA and, 36
  rules for, 16, 20
  women's, 39–40, 41
Cooper, Chuck, 31
Cooper, Cynthia, 81–83

court size and markings, 12–13
Cousy, Bob, 50–51

D

Dallas Mavericks, 34
defensive play, 24–25, 26
Denver Nuggets, 35
Detroit Pistons, 33, 74
Douglas, Robert, 28
draft, basketball, 36
dribbling, 18, 20

E

Eastern Conference, 33–34
  Atlantic Division, 33
  Central Division, 33–34
  Southeast Division, 34
Erving, Julius, 48, 59–60

F

fast-break style, 26
Fédération Internationale de Basketball, 45
fouls, 20, 22–24, 27
  personal, 22, 24
  technical, 24
free throw line, 13, 18
free throws, 18, 24, 27

G

goaltending, 20
Golden State Warriors, 36

H

Harlem Globetrotters, 28, 29, 42, 53, 80
high school basketball
  court for, 12, 13
  fouls and, 24
  recruiting for NBA and, 36
  rules for, 16, 20
  women's, 39, 41
hook shot, 22
Houston Comets, 81, 83
Houston Rockets, 34

I

Indiana Pacers, 33, 42, 63
international basketball, 12, 16, 20, 38, 44–47
International Women's Sports Federation, 40

J

Jackson, Phil, 70, 72, 73
James, LeBron, 75–77
Johnson, Magic, 31–32, 48, 62, 63–66

Jones, K.C., 51
Jordan, Michael, 32, 48, 66–70
jump shot, 22

K

Knight, Bobby, 62

L

Lapchick, Joe, 28
layup, 21
Lieberman, Nancy, 42–43, 79–81
Lloyd, Earl, 31
Los Angeles Clippers, 36
Los Angeles Lakers, 36, 53, 55, 58, 63, 65, 66, 70, 72, 73–75

M

Malone, Karl, 69
man-to-man defense, 26, 28
Memphis Grizzlies, 35
Meyers, Ann, 42
Miami Heat, 34, 72, 75, 77
Mikan, George, 29, 48–50
Miller, Cheryl, 81
Milwaukee Bucks, 33, 56, 58
Minneapolis Lakers, 29, 50

Minnesota Timberwolves, 35
motion offense, 25–26

N

Naismith, James, 10–12, 27, 40, 48
National Basketball Association (NBA)
court for, 13
early years of, 29–31
era of superstars in, 31–32
fouls and, 24
international players in, 47
notable players, 48–83
rules for, 15, 16, 20
today, 32–37
WNBA and, 44
National Basketball Development League (NBDL), 36
National Basketball League, 27, 29
National Collegiate Athletic Association (NCAA), 41, 55, 58, 62, 65, 68
New Jersey Nets, 33
New Orleans Hornets, 35
New York Knicks, 33
New York Renaissance (Rens), 28–29

O

offensive play, 24–26
Oklahoma City Thunder, 35
Olympics
    basketball in the, 45, 52,
        55, 65–66, 68, 75, 77
    women's basketball in,
        40, 43, 79, 81
O'Neal, Shaquille, 70–72,
    73–75
one-hand push shot, 22
Original Celtics, 28
Orlando Magic, 34,
    70–72, 75
out-of-bounds, awarding
    ball, 22, 24

P

Philadelphia 76ers, 33,
    53, 59
Philadelphia Warriors, 53
Phoenix Mercury, 80, 83
Phoenix Suns, 35, 72
pick-and-roll, 25–26
play-offs, 36
Portland Trail Blazers, 35
press defense, 26

R

referees, 16
Robertson, Oscar, 55–56
Russell, Bill, 51–52

S

Sacramento Kings, 36, 52
salaries, players', 37
San Antonio Spurs, 34, 77
Saperstein, Abe, 29
Seattle SuperSonics, 52
Sharman, Bill, 51
shot clock, 20
slam dunk, 22, 60
Stern, David, 31
Stockton, John, 66
Swoopes, Sheryl, 83

T

Thompson, Tina, 83
three-point line, 13, 18
three-point shot, 18, 24, 31
Title IX, 41
Toronto Raptors, 33

U

United States Basketball
    League, 43, 80
Utah Jazz, 35

V

violations, 20–22

W

Washington Wizards,
    34, 69

Western Conference, 34–36
   Northwest Division, 35
   Pacific Division, 35–36
   Southwest Division,
     34–35
Women's American
   Basketball Association
   (WABA), 80
women's basketball,
   38–44, 46, 79–83
   development of, 38–39
   rise of the WNBA, 41–44
   rules for, 39
Women's Basketball
   League (WBL), 80

Women's National
   Basketball
   Association
   (WNBA), 44, 79–83
Women's Professional
   Basketball League,
   41–42
Woodard, Lynette, 42
World Amateur
   Basketball
   Championship, 40

Z

zone defense, 26